ARS GEOMANTICA

FOUNDATIONS OF PRACTICAL SORCERY VOLUME III

FOUNDATIONS OF PRACTICAL SORCERY VOLUME III

ARS GEOMANTICA

BEING AN ACCOUNT AND RENDITION OF THE ARTE OF
GEOMANTIC DIVINATION AND MAGIC

Gary St. M. Nottingham

Published by Avalonia
www.avaloniabooks.co.uk

Published by Avalonia

BM Avalonia
London
WC1N 3XX
England, UK
www.avaloniabooks.co.uk

ARS GEOMANTICA
Copyright © 2012 Gary St. Michael Nottingham

First Edition 2012.
This revised edition, 2015.

All rights reserved.

ISBN 978-1-905297-76-4

Design by Satori, for Avalonia.

British Library Cataloguing in Publication Data. A catalogue record for this book is available from the British Library.

All rights reserved. No part of this publication may be reproduced or utilised in any form or by any means, electronic or mechanical, including photocopying, microfilm, recording, or by any information storage and retrieval system, or used in another book, without written permission from the author.

About the Author

Gary St. M. Nottingham's commitment to the study and practice of the alchemical arte, ritual magic, grimoires and spirit conjuration means that he can often be found peering at bubbling flasks or a shewstone – or otherwise engaged in deepening his knowledge and understanding of such matters. His practices also draw on the work of the 17th-century astrologer William Lilly and the arte of horary astrology.

Gary was raised in south Shropshire, where, during his mid-teens, he became involved with a small Coven, thereby gaining an excellent grounding in a wide selection of magical practices. Following the conjuration of a spirit, and asking it for help that manifested when least expected, he subsequently became involved with a group of practising alchemists. He has a background in horticulture, enjoys spending time in the garden and playing chess. He organised the legendary Ludlow Esoteric Conference (2004-2008), helped produce *Verdelet* occult magazine, has taught many free day workshops on basic occult skills and is a popular speaker at esoteric conferences.

The seven volumes of *Foundations of Practical Sorcery* are an unabridged collection of Gary's much sought-after previously published work, updated and made available to a wider readership at last.

For Mary

Table of Contents

INTRODUCTION 8

FREE WILL OR DESTINY? 11
INSTRUMENTS OF ARTE 14
GEOMANTIC SYMBOLS OF ARTE 16
BIRTHING THE SYMBOLS OF ARTE 25
BENDING THE BENDABLE 33
'AS I DO WILL SO MOTE IT BE!' 41
'DOORS OF PERCEPTION' 60

INDEX 65

Introduction

We live in an age where we are awash with information on all subjects, and to this the magical artes are no exception. Whilst the student of magic can easily access all manner of electronic files there is nothing quite like a book.

A book can not only be picked up and read, but will, in many instances, over time, become a friend, guide and teacher who has assisted the reader on their journey throughout their life. Quite simply books can change lives and this is why those who have been in positions of power through the centuries have tried, and often failed, to keep knowledge out of the hands of everyday folk. This is perhaps primarily because they feared the power of the book to cause change, and change is what the seven books in the Foundations of Practical Sorcery series will cause.

Today the magical artes have never been so accessible, although that doesn't mean the demands that the arte makes upon the practitioner have been lessened in any way. While the arte is, in principle, for all, not everyone will have the self-discipline, the will and the imagination to succeed therein. However for those who do have these basic attributes or are prepared to acquire them there is much to be gained from the practice of magic in all levels of life. For many people their ingress into the arte will be by books, and the exploration of and working with the information they contain. There is nothing like experience even if your magic proves less successful than hoped for: there is no such thing as failure in magic, because every experience will, at the very least, teach the practitioner something, even if it's just to try harder next time!

Of course some will have access to a magical group and the knowledge and collective experience to be found therein; but for many this will not be the case. Magical groups regardless of hue by and large have much to commend them, but not all of them do. I have in the past been approached by people who have gone through a coven system yet then been led to ask me to help them practice and study magic. It seemed their coven did not in fact practice the arte; which left me wondering what was it that they did do. I am aware of similar approaches made to other magical practitioners, which has left me concluding that some magical groups and covens can actually be detrimental to an individual's magical development and understanding - although this is certainly not the case with all by any means.

Foundations of Practical Sorcery goes some way to rectifying this deficit in any student's magical life. They offer clear magical instruction and accounts of magical acts to be performed, thus making the arte easily accessible. The methods and techniques presented are all based upon my own personal knowledge and experience which goes back over forty years, methods and techniques that have worked successfully for me and will do so for any reader who applies them accordingly.

In many ways I was fortunate, during the autumn of 1972, to meet a magical practitioner who taught me much regarding the arte, generously affording me the run of their magical library as well. Having been schooled extensively in magical knowledge from my mid teen years I consider myself to have been extremely fortunate and lucky to have had many experiences not easily available to many people. Thus the present Foundations of Practical Sorcery series is the distillation of four decades of successful magical workings.

Each of the seven volumes gives a clear account and rendition of one or another area of magical instruction that I have received and have been taught. They are presented to the reader in a clear and workable style which will provide them with a concise and firm foundation, allowing the serious magical student to explore the Western Magical Tradition, the inheritance of us all.

Gary St. M. Nottingham, February 2015

CHAPTER ONE

Free Will or Destiny?

Sometime in the latter years of BCE, the fledgling Roman state was at war with the might of Carthage, who were their main rival for the domination of the Mediterranean area. This was a fight that Rome needed to win, as the victor would be granted complete control of the Mediterranean trade routes. Rome had assembled a great fleet that was prepared for war, a fleet that was keen and eager to grapple with the Carthaginian forces that were on their way. Pompey, the Roman commander, stood on the sea-shore and waited. The priests brought forth the sacred chickens to divine the outcome of the coming battle. Grain was, with suitable invocations, sprinkled on the ground and the chickens were set loose.

If they ate the grain then all would be well, if not... Suddenly the cry went up, *'The sacred chickens were off their food!'* Not a good omen. With fury Pompey picked up the chickens and threw them into the sea saying, 'If they won't eat then let them drink!' The chickens drowned and Pompey subsequently led his troops to defeat. Ever since the dawn of time people have wanted to know what was going to happen, and humanity being what it is, has in various cultures and at various times, created innumerable schemas of divination to perceive the mind of God.

Is everything therefore predestined and subsequently not worth bothering about, because you cannot change it? I would answer both Yes and No, which I realise is not helpful. It is said that a *'Fool is governed by his stars but a wise man rules them.'* The natural flow of your life's energies will take you in the direction that you are going, and it will take an act of will to change it. Because of whom you are and the experiences that you have had, you may not feel up to changing things. However there will be those who will summon up their courage and the energies to do so, and if the potential of your birth chart indicates that you could go in a certain direction then it is going to be easier for you to do so. If there is no potential for the achieving of your aims that must be accepted and other options will need to be considered.

Fate will bring you to a variety of crossroads as you go through life, with each path giving you a valid experience. Some paths will bring you in a roundabout way to other points that you could have reached if you had taken a different path. This may be long and arduous or not so. All will be valid, because you have an element of free will to exercise. If a river flows in one direction, one may claim that it is following its natural path back to its source. For example the river could be dammed and re-directed, to do so someone has to exercise their will to enable this to happen. By an act of will you could do the same, having seen the natural flow of events in your life you could be the instigator of your life's patterns and not the victim. But this will take an act of will. There are many reasons why we do not, some are because we are lazy and weak, or simply that we are just stupid.

The reasons why we accept our supposed fates are legion, some are seen as valid, others less so. With divination there is always the subjectivity of the diviner to take into consideration. It is easy to give the answer that you want, and to influence the outcome by your own needs and wants. Of the various divinatory systems in existence, both geomancy and horary astrology can give the inquirer a clear yes or no answer. Both systems can be expanded to give a more detailed answer to the question asked. Of them both, geomancy is the easiest to learn and the quickest to use, although it does use an astrological schema in its practice. Geomancy is not feng shui nor is it ley-lines; it is an ancient Western Tradition which has had little or no interest from the New Age or Pagan community. It is a system that is based on sixteen geomantic figures, that have been generated from counting up the dots which have been made in the soil with a stick or on a piece of paper with a pen, that has been reserved solely for the arte. Some will use a dice and count the subsequent dots. All will work equally well. Geomancy was probably at its height during the Middle Ages and Renaissance years, having been introduced into Europe by Arabic influences.

Both Agrippa and Robert Fludd, who were important occult writers of their day, were instrumental in popularising the arte through their writings on the subject. So did John Heydon, who was writing on occult matters during the 17th century, the years of the *'English Magical Renaissance.'* He was considered in some quarters as the *'English Plagiarist,'* due to his habit of publishing other people's work as his own.

However, apart from living with Nicholas Culpeper's wife after

Culpeper's death and helping to publish some of his work, he is primarily remembered for his work *Theomagia, 'The Temple of Wisdom'*. This became popular amongst the 18th and 19th century occult classes because of its wealth of geomantic information and is still of relevance today. Whilst geomancy uses an astrological classification within its modus, geomancy was decidedly more reliable than the astrology of that time, as astrology would have been hampered by the lack of accurate timekeeping; a problem which did not affect geomancy. The symbols of geomancy, which are of the essence of simplicity to generate, can be expanded upon by using astrological praxis to grant a more in-depth view of the situation inquired of. They can also be used within magical praxis as doorways to explore other levels of consciousness, and also for spell workings and talismans, more so if used with animating fluids to influence the outcome of events - see *'Bending the Bendable.'*

CHAPTER TWO

Instruments of Arte

The arte of geomantic praxis is the generation and the accurate interpretation of its symbols. As already mentioned, the symbols can be generated by diverse methods. In modern times, in answer to the traditional geomantic modus operandi, whereby the symbols were birthed by making a line of dots in the ground with a pointed stick at random and then counting them up, modern practitioners of this venerable arte will use a pen and paper to do the same. You could if you so wished to, proceed in this manner, if you do then have a pen solely dedicated to the geomantic arte and used for no other purpose. Others may prefer to use a more arcane method from traditional witchcraft. This technique is equally simple as the pen and paper method.

On a waxing moon early in the morning, take yourself off to a hazel tree that you have already become acquainted with. You must explain to the tree that you require some of its wood to make your geomantic rune sticks. If it feels right and the omens are favourable, then with a clean cut with your knife of arte cut a suitable branch about three foot long.

Leave payment for the branch in the form of a coin or some milk, grain, honey or some of your life force on the ground under the tree. The rod must now be peeled and cut into four equal staves and carved flat on both sides along its length. In the middle of the stave paint with black paint a dot, on the other side of the stave paint two black dots. When the paint is dry, the staves must be sprinkled with the waters of the arte and censed accordingly. They will also have to be kept wrapped up in a dark cloth, silk would be ideal, the staves must be kept out of sight of cowans; that is the uninitiated into our arte and those who are ignorant and unsympathetic of our praxis, for let their sneers and jeers be made manifest in their own lives and not ours. To en-hallow and make holy your staves of knowing you must wait until the night of the full moon, better if lunar inhabits airy signs such as Libra, Aquarius or Gemini, but this is not strictly necessary. In your place of working enkindle some incense, preferably of a mercurial nature, as the staves are being dedicated for the finding out of answers to questions asked.

If you do not have anything suitable to hand then use church incense or frankincense. When you have gathered your staves and regalia together, face the eastern quarter and visualise above your head a glowing ball of divine brilliance, place your right hand therein and draw down the light through the crown of your head and let it flow the length of your body until it reaches your feet, at this point touch your chest with your right hand.

Now touch your right shoulder and as you bring your hand over to touch your left shoulder see a brilliant line of light travelling across your body from your right shoulder unto your left shoulder; thus making a cross of light with its centre at your heart region. Cross your hands over this point and contemplate again the brilliance above your head and let it flood your aura. Having placed some water in your chalice say:

> *'Hear me, O spirit of water My words I say*
> *For in thy presence no wight or phantasm stay.*
> *Hear my words I address to thee*
> *For this my will so Mote It Be!'*

This can also be used for the salt if the wording is changed accordingly. Then pour the salt into the water and sprinkle the staves with the water in the knowledge that anything of a malign nature is being washed away. By the flicker of the shimmering candle light, as the staves are held in the scented plume of burning incense, watch them glimmer and shine with the invoked energies. See them play around your staves and be absorbed by them.

If you do not wish to use staves or the pen and paper method, then find four pebbles, and on one side paint one dot and two dots on the other side, and follow the en-hallowing pattern here given or one of your own choosing. Wrap your stones or staves up in their cloth and put them away, only bring them out when they are to be used for divination. For they now belong to a different order and they are not of this everyday world and therefore they cannot be treated as such. Perform the opening gesture of the cross that you did at the beginning of the work to close.

CHAPTER THREE

Geomantic Symbols of Arte

There are sixteen geomantic symbols and each one has a specific meaning attached to them with astrological considerations that also have to be taken into account.

The sixteen geomantic symbols are:-

PUER (boy)

This is a figure of rashness, violence and energy and it is also destructive. It is considered unfavourable in all matters except in love and war. It is good in the third and sixth house but it is bad in the fifth (See astrological houses chapter four). The individual concerned is troublesome, passionate and excitable. They will also pursue sexual pleasure at the expense of all other considerations. Its planet is Mars and it rules the sign of Aries. Its magical image is the sword, although the sign is sometimes depicted as a man with large testicles. The element associated with it is fire and the incense is dragon's blood. Its spirit is Bartzabel.

Talismanic sigils:

AMISSIO (loss)

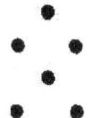

Although this is a figure of loss, it is good in questions of love. It represents a situation that is generally outside your grasp and is therefore unfavourable for gain. It is a figure that is favoured in the fifth and eighth houses but it is unfavoured in the second house. The planet of the sign is Venus and the house associated with the symbol is Taurus and the element is earth. The character of the person in a geomantic chart that it represents is somebody concerned with honour, but who will also stretch a point in their favour if they can get away with it. They are blunt in speech and can often be tactless; they are also prone to being quickly angered. The magical image of this sign is of a bag that is being held so that its mouth is pointing downwards and therefore its contents are falling out. The incense is rose and its spirit is Kedemel.

Talismanic sigils:

ALBUS (white)

This is a figure of peace, wisdom and purity; whilst it is a favourable figure in many circumstances it is however weak in action. Traditionally it has been considered good for profit and beginnings of any kind. It does well in the first and fourth house of a chart. The individual represented by this is peaceful and honest and has a charitable nature, but they are shy and can also be extravagant when spending money. The magical image is an upright goblet. The planet associated with it is Mercury and the astrological sign is Gemini. All mercurial odours such as mace or lavender are its perfumes. The spirit of the sign is Taphtharatharath and the element is air.

Talismanic sigils: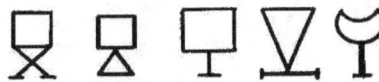

POPULUS (people)

● ●
● ●
● ●
● ●

This is a sign of gatherings and people. It is a neutral figure that is good with good and bad with bad. It is favoured in the tenth and third houses and it is unfavourable in the eighth. It is a sign that represents someone who is keen on travel and does not like to stay too long in one place. The magical image is a crowd of people and its planet is the moon. The astrological sign is Cancer and the element is water. The incense associated with this sign is jasmine and its spirit is Chasmondai.

Talismanic sigils:

FORTUNA MAJOR (greater fortune)

● ●
● ●
 ●
 ●

This is a symbol of good fortune, particularly of beginnings. It is a symbol of power and success and is favourable to the outcome of any contest. It is good in the first, fifth, sixth, ninth and eleventh houses; but is evil in the seventh house. Although the individual is frivolous with money, they are ambitious, generous and honest. Its planet is the Sun and its sign is Leo. The element that is associated with it is fire. The magical image that is of this sign is a valley through which flows a river. The incense for magical use is frankincense and the spirit is Sorath.

Talismanic sigils:

CONJUNCTIO (conjunction)

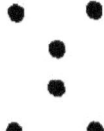

This is good for the recovery of lost things and it is favourable for good, particularly if it is with good figures. The sign is favoured in the first, seventh, ninth and tenth houses, but is considered to be ill-favoured in the eighth and twelfth houses. Its character is one of intelligence and eloquence, however the native can be ingenious but dishonest and they are likely to overspend. Its magical image is a crossroads. The governing planet is Mercury and it is of the astrological sign Virgo. The element that is associated with this sigil is earth and the spirit is Taphthartharath. All mercurial incenses belong to this sign.

Talismanic sigils:

PUELLA (girl)

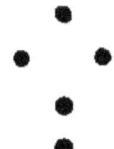

This is a sign of harmony and happiness. It is favourable for most questions but it can be fickle. It is a sign of emotion and passions. People characterised by this figure fall easily in and out of love, they are also quick to anger and they are intensely aware of their appearances. Venus rules this sign and it is associated with the astrological sign of Libra and the element air. Musk is its perfume as are all Venusian odours. The spirit is Kedemel with the magical imagery associated with this sigil being that of a mirror or sometimes a figure with large breasts.

Talismanic sigils:

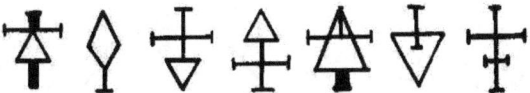

RUBEUS (red)

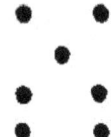

This is a figure of violence, vice and passion in all things. It is considered good in all that is evil and evil in all that is good. If it appears in the first house of the chart then the chart is not to be judged at that time. Whilst the sigil is good in both the sixth and the eighth houses, it is evil in the second, fourth and seventh house. The planet associated with it is Mars and the astrological sign is Scorpio, with the element water also being associated with it. Opopanax or Dragon's Blood are the incenses of this sigil and the magical imagery is of a goblet that is turned upside down. The spirit of the sigil is Bartzabel.

Talismanic sigils:

ACQUISITIO (gain)

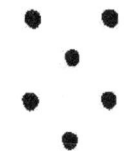

This sigil is a figure of success and gain, it relates to the success of all endeavours and enterprises. It is good for gain in all matters. It is favoured in the first, second, tenth and eleventh houses. The individual concerned is fussy about their appearance and they are stubborn. Jupiter is the planet of this sign and Sagittarius is the astrological sign, the element is fire. Cedar is the incense and the magical imagery is that of a bag with its mouth open and held upwards to receive. The spirit of the sigil is Hismael.

Talismanic sigils:

CARCER (prison)

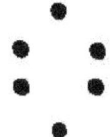

This sign is unfavourable except for questions relating to stability or security. It however represents stability and restrictions, delays, binding and imprisonment. The character of this sigil is someone who is fierce and passionate, however they can be magnanimous. The planet of the sigil is Saturn and the astrological sign is Capricorn, with the element being earth. Myrrh is the incense and the magical image is of an enclosure. The spirit is Zazel.

Talismanic imagery:

TRISTITIA (sorrow)

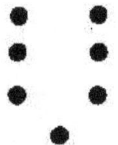

This is a sign that represents suffering, sorrows and illness. It is unfavourable in all questions except for those relating to buildings or those that are concerned with the earth. The individual that this sigil refers to will be one who is dishonest and quick to anger, they will be slow to laugh or to forgive or forget. It is unfavourable in all houses except for the fourth and eighth. The magical imagery is a stake with its point driven downwards and the incense is civet or myrrh. The spirit is Zazel and the astrological sign is Aquarius, with air being its element and Saturn its planet.

Talismanic sigils:

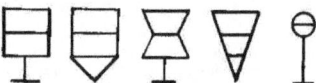

LAETITIA (joy)

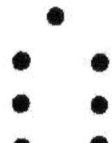

This is a figure of happiness and health. It is favourable in all questions. It is good in the fifth and eleventh houses and ill favoured in the sixth, eighth and twelfth houses. Its character is one of intelligence and honesty and is often good natured and religious. Magical image is of a tower and the planet is Jupiter, with the astrological sign being Pisces. The element is water and the incense is cedar, with the spirit being Hismael.

Talismanic sigils:

CAUDA DRACONIS (tail of the dragon)

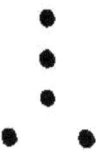

This is an unfavourable figure that brings good with evil and evil with good. It is good for loss or endings. Its character is corrupt and dangerous. It is favoured in the sixth, ninth and twelfth houses and is unfavourable in the second, fourth and eleventh. It is the south node of the Moon a1st line of first mother nd is associated with the element fire. Its incense is a blend of dragon's blood and myrrh. Its magical imagery is of a door with footsteps leading away from it.

Talismanic sigils:

CAPUT DRACONIS (head of the dragon)

This figure is good for beginnings and for profit; it is good with good figures and bad with bad figures. It is good in the second and seventh houses but bad in the twelfth house. Its character is good, faithful and honest. The planet is the north node of the Moon; it is associated with the element earth. The traditional magical image is a doorway with foot prints leading up to it. The incense is a mixture of rose and cedar.

Talismanic sigils:

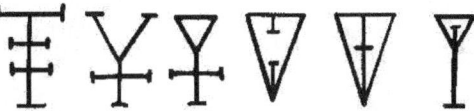

FORTUNA MINOR (lesser fortune)

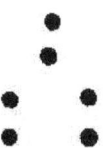

This is a figure of change and instability. It is good for things that are required to be done quickly; its character is bold and presumptuous but can be generous and honest. It is favoured in the eighth and ninth houses but not in the second. Its planet is the Sun and Leo is the astrological sign associated with this sigil. Air is its element and Sorath its spirit. The magical image is a hilltop on which is placed a pole. The incense is solar such as frankincense.

Talismanic sigils:

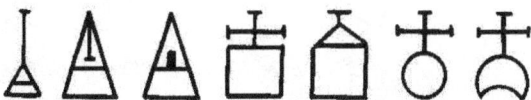

VIA (way)

Whilst this figure is unfavourable in most things it is good for journeys. This sign represents change between good and bad fortunes. Its character is one of frequent change with a liking to be on the move. Those whom it represents are slow to anger but when aroused they can be dangerous. The Moon is connected to this sigil and so is the astrological sign Cancer. The spirit is Chasmondai and the incense is white sandalwood and camphor. The magical image is a road, with water being its element.

Talismanic sigils:

CHAPTER FOUR

Birthing the Symbols of Arte

Fetch forth from their lair the staves of knowing, unwrap them and let them greet the world. Contemplate your question and lay out the cloth that the staves have been housed in and let this be your work surface. Taking one stave at a time spin it between your palms and let it drop on to the cloth whilst you concentrate on the question. Note how many dots are facing you on the stave when it is lying down on the cloth. If it is an odd number then make one dot on a piece of paper, if it is an even number then make two dots on the paper. With the second stave do the same and so with the third and fourth staves. Place the resultant dots in order under the first dot so that they are in a row going downwards.

This operation of the arte will have to be repeated three more times altogether to give a total of four figures. These four figures are referred to as the Mothers and are those from whom all other figures will be generated. To illustrate this point I give the following figures which will obviously differ from any given operation of this arte that you may undertake.

1st Mother	2nd Mother	3rd Mother	4th Mother
• • • • • •	• • • • •	• • • • • • •	• • • • • •

Next we birth the four daughters from the four mothers, which are done thus. The first line of each mother will create the first daughter, the second lines will give the second daughter, whilst the third lines will create the third daughter and the fourth and final lines will give the fourth daughter as demonstrated below.

1st Daughter	2nd Daughter	3rd Daughter	4th Daughter
• • • • • • •	• • • • • •	• • • • • • •	• • • • • •

From these daughters come the granddaughters or as they are sometimes known, the nieces. These figures are brought into being by adding together the dots of the first and second Mothers to create the first niece. Then add the dots of the third and fourth Mothers to create the second niece. The same is done with the first and second daughter, who will create the third niece, and the third and fourth daughter to create the fourth niece. Thus the dots of the first line of the first and second figures will create between them the first line of the first niece when they are added together, three being an odd number will grant one dot; even numbers will give two dots.

1st line of first mother, 2nd line of first mother; which creates the 1st line of the 1st niece.

1st Mother	2nd Mother
• •	•

1st line of the 1st niece
•

The 2nd line of the 1st mother with the 2nd line of the 2nd mother will give the 2nd line of the 1st niece thus:

1st Mother	2nd Mother
•	•

2nd line 1st Mother   2nd line 2nd Mother

When these are added together they will create the 2nd line of the 1st niece thus:

2nd line of the 1st niece
• •

Following this pattern the 3rd line of the 1st mother will give, with the 3rd line of the 2nd mother the 3rd line of the first niece.

1st Mother	2nd Mother
• •	• •

3rd line of 1st Mother   3rd line of the 2nd Mother

Which will create the 3rd line of the 1st niece:

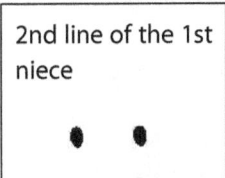

3rd line of the 1st niece
● ●

Finally the 4th line of the 1st mother and the 4th line of the 2nd mother will grant the 4th line of the 1st niece.

1st Mother	2nd Mother
●	●

4th line of 1st Mother 4th line of 2nd Mother

4th line of the 1st niece
● ●

The first niece is therefore created as thus:

```
   ●
 ●   ●
 ●   ●
 ●   ●
```

Laetitia

The other three nieces are as follows:

    2nd niece   3rd niece   4th niece

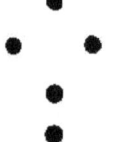 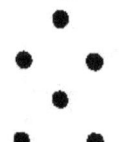 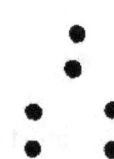

If we add together, as previously shown, the lines of the 1st and the 2nd nieces this will create a figure which is referred to as the 1st witness. The 3rd and 4th niece when added together will create the 2nd witness. When the two witnesses are added together themselves we get the Judge who will decide the outcome of the question asked. If it is a good figure then the answer is positive, if a bad figure then the answer will be negative.

2nd witness	1st witness	Judge

The first witness will refer to the past and the second witness will suggest how things will go. The judge in this example is Acquisitio, which means gain, therefore granting a positive outcome to the question asked. If a good judge is made from two good witnesses, then it is a clear yes answer and all will be well with little difficulty. When the judge is created from two bad figures then it is a clear no. However if the judge is made from a good first witness and a bad second witness it is clear that that which is asked about has started off well but has declined. A good judge however, if made from a bad figure can still suggest a good outcome but flawed in some way.

If a bad first witness is followed by a good second witness, then the question propounded has started badly but will end on a positive note, even if the judge is negative; a good second witness can mitigate some of the adverse effects of the judge. Whilst this system can produce a quick and accurate assessment of a given situation it can also be expanded into giving a more detailed account of what is going on. Furthermore, placing of the figures into a chart based on the house placements of medieval astrology we can expand our working giving a more detailed account with a clear assessment of that which is enquired about. This allows for a fuller picture of the question asked about to emerge; which will be helpful in gaining a clearer understanding.

House placements and where the figures dwell:

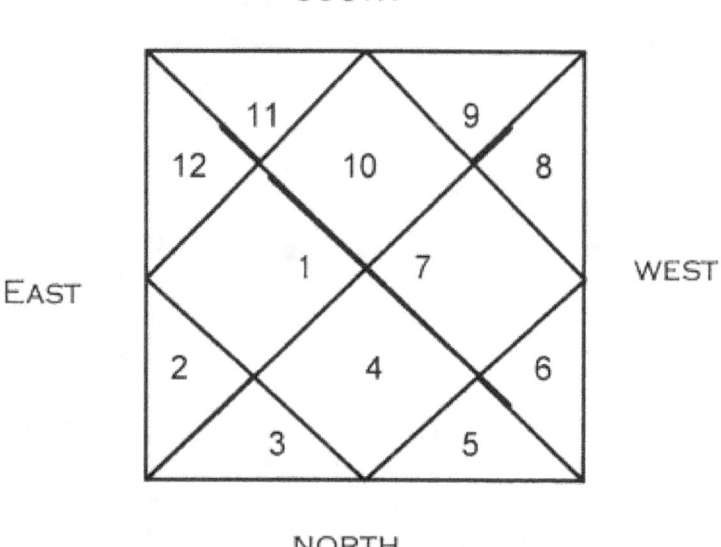

The first figure, that is the first Mother, dwells in the tenth house. The second Mother is placed in the first house, the third Mother is placed in the fourth house and the fourth Mother is attributed to the seventh house. These are the angular houses in astrology where placements act the most strongly. The first daughter is placed in the eleventh house, the second daughter in the second house, whilst the third daughter is in the fifth house and the fourth daughter in the eighth house. These are the succeedent houses of astrology and are weaker than the angular houses.

Finally the nieces dwell in the following houses: the first niece goes in the twelfth house, the second niece is placed in the third house, the third niece in the sixth house and lastly the fourth niece resides in the ninth house. These are the cadent houses where figures are at their weakest, except for Carcer and Tristitia who both excel themselves in cadent houses, being of the nature of Saturn.

The Houses of the Chart:

1st house: Deals with the querent, that is the person asking the question and it will describe them in some way.

2nd house: Querent's money and moveable goods. Of importance in tracing lost property.

3rd house: Brothers and sisters, short journeys, news, rumours, trade and publications.

4th house: Father, the grave and the end of the matter. Sibling's money, land, houses and property.

5th house: Games of chance, entertainments, children, sex. Father's money or moveable goods.

6th house: Health, animals, smaller than a goat. Money that belongs to your children. Uncles and aunts.

7th house: Wife, partner, friends and known enemies, father's death, also his property.

8th house: Wills, taxes, social security benefits, wife's finance. Death and occult matters.

9th house: Long journeys, education, church matters and the law.

10th house: The Mother, your public standing and job, people in general, the masses, the price of any property that is being sold or rented. Doctors and their medicines.

11th house: Your hopes and wishes, friends, mother's money.

12th house: Witchcraft, hospitals, your own undoing. Unknown enemies, animals larger than a goat. Imprisonment and restrictions.

The judgement:

Firstly look to the house that governs your question, if it is a question about your money then your money will be governed by the second house. If you have a good figure in the second house then all is well, not so if a bad figure dwells therein. Using the schema from astrology look to see what supports the house or hinders it. Figures that are sextile or trine are good, more so if trine. Bad aspects are the squares and opposition; opposition being more powerful. How is this worked out? Figures that are two houses apart from the one that is inquired about are sextile, which in astrological terms would be 60 degrees apart; this is good and helpful.

Those figures that are three houses away from that which is being asked about are square, not good and are unhelpful. This would be 90 degrees in astrological terms. Those figures that are four houses away are trine, which is good and most helpful; this would be 120 degrees apart. Finally any figure that is opposite, 180 degrees, is very bad and will prevent things going well. Therefore if a good or bad figure falls in these sensitive points help or hindrance will be indicated and how it will manifest.

For example, if the question is about money see what is in the opposite house. If a good figure, then no problems from that quarter, if it is a bad figure what is it telling you? For that you will have to consider the properties of the house and the figure that is in there. If good figures are in the fourth house along either side then good will come from that quarter. This is the same for all placements. Sextile or squares. What helps – what hinders? Whilst this formula can be expanded and be made even more complex, the salient features of the system which I have given above will more than amply provide you with a quick and accurate divination system, for all questions that you are likely to want to know the answer to.

CHAPTER FIVE

Bending the Bendable

One little known but pertinent method of spell casting is by using the geomantic sigils that belong to each figure. These symbols can be charged with your will and let loose in the world to accomplish your bidding accordingly. Whether for good or ill I make no judgement. I feel that the modern Wiccan Rede, *'An it harm none – Do what thou will,'* is no more than a piece of invented nonsense; of course others may very well disagree.

Whilst I am not encouraging you to wreak havoc at will, as there seems to me to be little point in adding to the world's store of misery needlessly, I am however not shying away from the fact that sometimes it may be deemed justified striking back. That is something that you will need to think about carefully, because if you were to go down that road there can be no turning back once magical energies have been set loose. Magical energies are like lightning, that is they take the shortest route to earth, so intent and will must be made abundantly clear, as subsequently you may end up with a situation that you hadn't bargained for and then what will you do? So always give the situation plenty of consideration.

Not all things can be influenced, but having said that a lot of things can be, you are endeavouring to *'bend the bendable,'* and you would do well to remember that you are not God. The sigils of our geomantic arte can and indeed are put to good magical practice.

Their energies can easily be accessed by constructing talismans, but they can also be used with fluid condensers, which are sometimes known to the wise as *'Philtron Animato,'* Anointing Philtres. These useful allies are conceived from various herbs and are extremely valuable in this type of magic, as they will hold energies as a storage battery and are quite easy to make and just need a little effort and practice. There is one condenser for each element, and one that is referred to as the Universal Condenser, which will do all that the elemental ones will do and more besides.

Ideally the elemental condensers are best brought into being when the Moon travels through an astrological sign which relates to the element concerned. For example when making a condenser for the air element wait until the Moon travels through an air sign such as Gemini, Libra or Aquarius and of course wait until a waxing Moon which can be found from an ephemeris.

Fire Condenser:

Preferably when the Moon travels through Aries, Leo or Sagittarius, take a clean kilner jar that has never been used. This is the wort cauldron, within whose belly will be conceived and birthed the fire condenser. Burn a little fire incense, frankincense mixed with dragon's blood would be ideal. State what your work is about and ask a blessing on your working. Take the jar and hold it in the rising incense smoke and let the suffumigations play both inside and on the outside of the jar in an act of dedication.

Now take the following herbs, which you have previously gathered together: garlic, onion, mustard and peppercorn and contemplate the fiery nature of them. Be careful of your eyes as this plant material is an irritant. Place the plants within the belly of the wort cauldron and cover with brandy. Pure alcohol from the grape would be ideal, brandy is a good substitute. The alcohol must be from the grape for alchemical reasons so do not use vodka, whisky or the like. Seal the jar tight and place it somewhere that is warm and dark where it can gestate in silence until the Moon returns back to the sign that it was in when you started the work. Strain the fluids off the marc and filter, keep separate the residue which can be taken outside and burnt, thus returning it to its element.

To this menstrum must be added several drops of aqua aurum, or gold water. This is simple to make and will be needed for the other three condensers as they will also need a few drops of this tincture added to them. Using clean water (not tap water; bottled water will do for this), heat a piece of gold, a ring will do, and when it is hot drop it into the water. This will splash so watch your eyes. The water can be poured off into a clean container and the gold reheated and the process repeated. By doing this several times minute particles of gold will be released into the water which will saturate it with its vibrations. This will be your gold water, and needs to be kept safe for future use. The fire menstrum can be kept in a dark bottle and kept somewhere safe and secret until needed.

Water Condenser:

Let the moon be in a watery sign such as Cancer, Scorpio or Pisces and treat the jar to house your menstrum according to the demands of our arte as previously shown, but use a water incense such as lotus oil or karaya gum. Failing all else resort to frankincense which is a good all-rounder. Place in the jar previously gathered herbs: the leaves or flowers of peony and willow, all water-borne plants will have an empathy with this element. Treat as before by placing them in the jar and covering them with brandy. Disperse the plant material after use by placing in a river or stream. Treat as the fire menstrum and when finished add some of your gold water to the tincture. Bottle and store safely away from prying eyes. Treated as such, these elemental menstrums are sensitive to the attitudes that are around them therefore it is better that they are not polluted by the adverse thoughts of the profane.

Air Condenser:

Let the Moon be in an airy sign such as Gemini, Libra or Aquarius, and place in a prepared jar as shown by examples already given, the following herbs and worts: hazel nuts or their leaves, coriander, juniper berries, and rose petals or leaves. Contemplate the nature of the element and ask a blessing on your work. Burn something suitable for the air element, such as galbanum or frankincense, cense the jar as before and place therein the gathered herbs and cover with brandy as before and some gold water, after it has been strained off and filtered. The plant material that is left over can be scattered to the winds to disperse. Seal and store safely until needed.

Earth Condenser:

Let the moon be domiciled in one of the following houses, Taurus, Virgo or Capricorn. Having gathered the following herbs: parsley (either root, seed or leaf), caraway seeds, carnation blooms, lemon balm and plantain leaves, place them in a clean jar that has been dedicated as our arte demands and as shown previously. Burn something earthy, such as patchouli or storax; or frankincense if nothing else is available. Spend some time contemplating the earth element and ask a blessing on the work in hand. As with the others place the herbs in the jar and cover with brandy. Seal and place in the darkness for the lunar month. Afterwards retrieve and separate from the marc, filter the fluids and bury that which is left over. The menstrum can now be poured, as the others were, into a dark bottle to which are added several drops of gold water.

Universal Fluid Condenser:

This one is as straightforward as the others are to produce, and will work on all levels. It is also useful for the creation of magical servants as described in *Liber Noctis*. It is potent in creating skrying fluids and for the empowerment of talismans and has many other magical applications which will aid one's magic.

Take at the full moon equal amounts of the following herbs which have been previously gathered: angelica, sage, lime flowers, cucumber, acacia leaves or gum, lily flowers, chamomile, cinnamon, nettles, poplar, violet flowers or leaves, peppermint, willow bark or leaves, dragon's blood and lavender flowers. If you have some astrological understanding, which all good sorcerers and witches should have, you could gather them on their planetary days in preparation for the full moon working, for which an ephemeris will be found useful.

Having gathered them, contemplate the working in hand and burn a little frankincense. With this incense suffume a clean jar, the wort cauldron, that will birth our worthy allies. Place the foregathered herbs therein and cover with brandy or better still pure alcohol. Seal the jar tightly and store away safely in the dark until the next full moon. Strain the tincture from the marc and place in a clean bottle. This is our fluid condenser, to which you must add some of the gold water previously mentioned.

The plant material must be burnt outside in a pot of some sort. This is best done on a camping stove or something that will give a high temperature. Let the remains be reduced to a grey ash, which should not take long. The ashes are now placed in a clean jar and are covered with clean water; bottled water or filtered rain water will be suitable. Shake regularly and the next day pour carefully off the ash. This water is now placed in a clean dish and gently evaporated. This will leave behind a white salt, although it may be slightly coloured. This salt can be further purified by repeating the process again, but for what we need, this much will suffice. At the full moon leave the dish outside under the light of the moon. By the morning the salts will be damp or have turned to water; this will depend on the state of their purity. The salts and moisture will have to be poured carefully into the fluid condenser; shake the bottle and store for a month in a warm place so that they can be quietly absorbed. This alchemical technique will grant further potency to your menstrum and can also be done for the four elemental condensers that you have produced. These condensers need to be treated as holy and kept out of the way of the profane.

Modus Operandi:

Each element has an area of influence and therefore they can be worked with to influence events accordingly. Their areas of influence are as follows:

Fire:

Good to work with for projects of creativity, one's maleness and matters of lust. It is also useful for works of protection and destruction.

Water:

Will influence all matters of love and friendship, fertility, joy and psychic receptivity.

Air:

Good for works of healing, travel and learning. Also for works of communication. Or dispersing someone or something, causing rows or bickering.

Earth:

Work with this element for all matters relating to finance, jobs and anything relating to the mundane world. Also good for blocking or binding someone or something.

To work with the fire element, first contemplate the fiery essence of creation and en-kindle some suitable incense. Take a clean piece of paper and cense with the intention that your magic will come to birth in accordance with your will. Write on the paper that which you are working for, remembering that this needs to be clear as to what it is that you mean, with no room for ambiguity. Pour on to the paper four drops of your fire condenser and gaze into the depths of the paper and see your will being accomplished, saying verbally to yourself that which you are working for.

Trace the fire pentagram over the working thus:

Hold the paper in the candle flame (a red candle would be ideal) and say as it burns:

> 'Hear Me, O fire For my will I say
> Release the spell this very day!
> Hear my words I address to thee
> For this my will So Mote It Be!'

Rhyming couplets are very good in such spell workings as they encompass the intent of the spell, which will help when releasing it into the subtle realms which are around us. Let the paper now burn out completely with the sure and certain knowledge that your will is being accomplished in the world. Do not doubt this as doubts are fateful to the success of your magic, if you doubt and do not have sure faith in the outcome then you will effectively undermine your magic, in fact you will be performing a counter spell to fail.

With the water element follow the same procedure, that is, contemplate the element that you are working with and burn if possible a little incense that again is suitable to the working in hand. Pour clean water into a chalice (do not use tap water) and into this drop four drops of the water condenser. Look into the depths of the water and again see your will coming to pass in the sure and certain knowledge that the future now has no escape from your will. Not easy but this certainty will help fire your intent into reality and will become easier with practice. Take the water to a pool or river outside and release it into its element and address the waters as such without being observed:

> *'Hear Me, O element water*
> *For my will I say etc'*

Again look into the waters and see the things that you are working for coming to pass.

With the air element there are two methods of working. the first is to write your will out on a piece of clean paper and add four drops of the air condenser onto the paper. The paper will need to be torn into pieces and thrown into the air on a windy day to disperse the spell. This is a good method to get rid of someone or something. The second method is to take a small metal bowl and pour some water therein with four drops of the condenser. Heat the bowl on an open flame and as the steam rises see therein your will coming to reality and as it does say:

> *'Hear Me, O element air For my will I say etc.'*

In both workings firstly endeavour to connect with the air element in some way; a short meditative practice would help as it would for all of the elemental workings that are given. And again burn some suitable incense as an aid to create the right atmosphere; this will help to promote a connection with the element concerned.

With the element of earth you will need to take a small bowl of earth or dig a hole outside into which you will need to drop some of your fluid condenser and repeat your rhyming couplets, whilst gazing into the depths of the soil and seeing your will coming to pass. Take the soil back outside and release it into its element. If you had dug a hole in the ground to work with, then fill it back in and as you walk away do not look back. I have known people to work with yew trees using this simple method.

Depending on what it is that you are working for you can visualise the geomantic symbols that relate to your chosen element either in their physical element that you are working with, or write them on the paper and release them through their element. The symbols can also be marked on a suitable candle, charged and lit so that their energies can be released. If you have a mirror that you use for magic you could place that on your altar, perform a suitable rite for the element involved and then trace the geomantic symbols appertaining to the working on the surface of the magic mirror with the fluid condenser.

With the use of suitable fluid condenser, invocations, wording and incense an effective rite can be performed. This will take some skill with concentration and visualisation which must be developed to an above average degree for your magic to work. Fortunately if it is weak, as it is with most people, it can be easily developed with persistence and practice. With this simple system there is plenty of scope for the rites to be developed into more complex workings should your sense of the arte so demand, or they can easily be adapted to the practices of modern witchcraft: there is boundless scope for the inventive. Such magic as this can take a lunar month to work depending on how much energy you are able to raise, and some workings will take more than one application depending on their complexities. But like water that drips on to a rock, with repetition and patience it will wear the rock away, which is itself a good lesson in magical development. Magic is a demanding arte that requires a determined soul to succeed therein, thus it is not for the many but for those who will make the effort required for success.

CHAPTER SIX

'As I Do Will So Mote It Be!'

Geomantic symbols and their energies can easily be accessed via the use of talismans. This versatile system of magic is well suited to the artes of geomancy. However this magical arte does require a more disciplined approach than those which we have worked with so far. All symbols have a life of their own and are physical representations of living energies on the subtle levels of creation. The symbols of our arte need to be treated with respect for they are potent and living beings.

Symbols, like emotions, are the language of the subconscious levels. The early 20th century magician Dion Fortune has in her teachings equated the subconscious with the subtle Kabbalistic levels of Yesod. In the Kabbalah, Yesod is the gateway to the worlds beyond and the higher levels. It is at this level that your magic must work first, to affect the world of the everyday. The energies that are beyond Yesod will answer to your call as it resonates in the unseen world. Summoned aright and with an undaunted will, they will ensoul the talisman and will then bring your magic to birth.

There are several methods to access and work with these energies of creation. Spirits can be bound to a talisman and only released when they have achieved your goal. Other methods will simply pour the divine powers that are aroused into the talisman; both methods will work well, with the latter method being the easier to work with. Magic within the Western Magical Tradition has various rituals for this type of work, some complex, others less so. However what they all have in common is a disciplined and determined approach; wishful thinking and a weak attitude will not engender success. You must focus on your will and keep it before you at all times - *'As I Do Will, So Mote It Be!'*.

Failure is not before you. It is this sure and certain attitude that will promote the inevitable success of your working, for then there can be no other outcome. The complexities of ceremonial magic can take a good while to learn and to absorb, but they can be highly effective and impressive to watch.

In the present instance we will use simple but equally effective methods from ceremonial magic to ensoul talismans. For positive change or gain one must remember to work on the waxing moon, for a negative outcome, or to banish, on the waning moon. The moon rules over the subtle tides of ebb and flow that flow through creation, and unless you are an adept you will be more successful if you work with these tides. As we are using geomantic symbols to create elemental talismans it would also be useful to work when the moon is passing through a house that is relevant to the element that we are working with. For example for earth workings use Taurus, Virgo or Capricorn symbols at a time when the moon is travelling through one of these houses.

The Lesser Banishing Ritual of the Pentagram (LBRP):

This is a useful rite to clear atmospheres prior to magical workings and will be found to aid the construction of your talismans. It is suitable as a daily rite that will help dispel the psychic flotsam and jetsam that hover within our vicinities. It is also powerful to quieten disturbed atmospheres. It can be expanded and used in various ways to achieve a variety of occult goals.

To perform this act of ceremonial magic, one must face the eastern quarters and still your mind. Concentrate on the area above your head, see a brilliant ball of light, and now with your hand raised into it bring your hand down to your forehead, touch it and intone the wording AH-TEH (*thou art*) whilst visualising that the light has travelled in a line down to your head. Now bring the light down through your body to your feet and as you do touch your breast and say MALKUTH (*the kingdom*). Touch your right shoulder and intone GEBURAH (*and the power*) and bring your hand over to your left shoulder and touch it, as you do saying GEDULAH (*and the glory*). See the light travel from your right to your left shoulder thus forming a cross of light within your being. Place the hands, crossed, upon the chest while intoning LE-OLHAM, AMEN (*forever and ever, Amen*). Still facing the eastern quarter trace in the air before you with your hand that has the first two fingers extended, the banishing pentagram of earth thus:

See it glow brightly, then stab the centre of it with your right hand and intone YHVH (yod-heh-vav-heh). Let it move out to the periphery of your work space and as it does so let it push back all negativity. Now with your right arm raised and pointing at the right arm of the pentagram trace a line of light around to the south. Here draw in the air before you as you did at the east another pentagram. The word here is ADNI (adoni). Bring the line around to the western quarter and again draw before you the pentagram; the word is EHIEH (eh-heh-eh). Finally bring the line around to the north and trace a final pentagram in the air before you; the word here is AGLA.

The line is continued around to the first pentagram in the east so that you now have a complete circle around you and a pentagram at each of the compass points. Visualise and hold these well.

Facing east stretch your arms out so that you form a cross and visualise a tall yellow robed figure in the eastern quarter facing you. Feel the element of air blowing from that quarter and intone, *'Before Me Raphael!'* Visualise behind you at the circle's edge but on the outside another tall blue robed figure holding a chalice. Intone *'Behind Me Gabriel!'* Feel the water flowing from this quarter, try and hear it running. Visualise on your right hand, again at the circle's edge, a tall, mighty, red robed figure. See flames playing around this figure who bears a sword and intone *'On my right hand Mikael!'* Finally see on your left hand at the circle's edge a tall sombre robed figure in the colours of the earth, standing in a corn field. Here intone whilst concentrating on the imagery *'On my left hand Auriel!'* Now a six-pointed star is visualised forming on your back, made of two interlacing triangles, as you declare, *'About me flame the pentagrams behind me shines the six-rayed star.'*

Then perform the opening gestures of the cross. When pronouncing the words try to lower slightly the pitch of one's voice so that it vibrates slightly in the chest cavity. This is the Lesser Banishing

Ritual of the Pentagram. Whilst it may seem a little daunting, daily practice will promote a more confident flow with it. We will use this rite at the beginning and at the ending of consecration rites.

To make and empower a talisman we must consider what element will serve our purpose best. Then when the moon is suitably placed in the heavens, we set to work. First create a clean and tidy work place, let the floor be swept clean with the intent that negativity is being banished from the working area. Using something that is suitable for your altar, which is the table before the high ones, let it face the east. Having washed and put on clean clothes or a robe, light the candles and incense, with the incense being something that is suitable for the work in hand. The candles can ideally be of the appropriate colour, like the altar cloth, although plain white will suffice. However if using colours then let yellow be for the air element, red for fire, blue for water and green for earth.

Anything that relates to the element that you are working with such as a stone for earth or feathers for air can be placed in the elemental quarter. Or place a lighted candle in that quarter. If you do so take care that you do not burn your house down which would be somewhat self defeating! On the altar, place a glass of water and some salt and the talisman, which is drawn on card or parchment in the colour of the element concerned. You can either pour a few drops of your condenser into the ink that you use or a couple of drops can be placed on the talisman itself and then left to dry. Some people will paint the parchment or card that will form the material body of the talisman and then let it dry before use.

When all is gathered and ready to proceed, ensure that you are not disturbed and take the phone off the hook and lock the door if possible. Having made certain in your mind that this is indeed your will, it can now be set loose in the world. Standing at the centre and facing east over the altar, which should be in the middle, perform the Lesser Banishing Ritual of the Pentagram. Pour the salt into your hand and trace over it a cross to en-hallow it. Salt does not need to be consecrated but blessed, as it is already holy, as it preserves by nature. As the cross is visualised say:

> 'I bless and dedicate
> This holy creature of salt unto the success of my magic.
> By the power of the God Most High and by mine own divinity.'

You could use suitable wording of your own to do this but the intent must be made clear. Pointing the first and second fingers of your right hand at the water, see the life force flow from your hand into the water and be absorbed by it. As you do say:

> 'For I consecrate thee O creature of water
> let all malignancy and hindrance be cast out here forth and let only good enter herein.
> Wherefore I do bless thee and consecrate thee (make sign of the equal-armed cross over the water) To the success of this my magic!
> By the power of the God Most High And by mine own divinity.
> So Mote It Be!'

Now pour the salt into the consecrated water. Starting in the east walk around the edge of your workspace desoil, that is sun-wise, and sprinkle some of the holy water around the edge of your circle and as you do so say:

> 'So therefore the Sorcerer/ess
> Who governeth the works of fire
> doth sprinkle with the waters of the loud resounding sea.'

Having completed the circuit place the glass of water on your altar and pick up the censer, starting in the east, cense the circle's edge whilst saying:

> 'And when all the phantoms have vanished thou shalt see the holy formless fire, that fire that flashes through the hidden depths of creation. Hear thou the voice of fire!'

Having completed your circuit place the censer on the altar and declare your work in hand. Always start your working with a general orison to divinity, as you are placing your working under the auspices of the highest. This can be one of your own devising or use the example that is given below:

> 'Blessed art thou Lord of Creation for thy power flows out
> unto the ends of being rejoicing.
> Be with me now as I perform this work and grant success unto my magical endeavours.'

Now follows an invocation unto the element concerned. For this use one of your own devising whilst facing the direction of the element in question. Gaze into the element's direction and see it being active. Again this invocation can be one of your own devising or use that which is given. (The God names and Archangelic names will be given for each element in due course):

> '*Hear Me O element of….* (state element) *for I invoke thine aid by the Mighty Names…* (God name)
> *and by the power of the Archangel… and the potency of the Angel…*
> *That the King of* (element), … (King's Name)
> *Will summon the realm of… (element) to assist me in this my Holy Act of Magic!*'

Note the order of the invocation, which starts with the God aspect of the element and it then follows a strict command on the descending hierarchies. This is because in the order that is given the world above will command the one below. Returning to the altar take the talisman and consecrate it with water saying as you do:

> '*O creature of talisman*
> *Let all malignancy be cast forth hence from so that only the holy power of…* (state element) *may enter here in.*
> *Wherefore I do bless, dedicate and consecrate thee in the Mighty Name God*
> *that thou do bring forth that which I do will!*
> *So Mote It Be!*'

Hold the talismanic figure in the rising incense smoke and as you cense the creature declare the following invocation.

> '*Further more by the potency of the Most High let this talisman be consecrated to the success of my will.*
> *Persist therein O holy…*(state element)
> *and rest not until my will is made manifest!*
> *So Mote It Be!*'

Let the talisman be placed on the altar top and breathe in deeply a few times and hold your mind blank for a few moments. Breathe in normally and as you do so, starting from your feet, imagine that each time that you breathe in, your body is starting to fill up with the element invoked. After several breaths you should be full to bursting with the element. Let the element be visualised in its colour and try to feel the sensations thereof.

When you are at this point intone either silently or verbally the God Name and the Archangel's name of the element in question for this and have no doubts that it could not be so, otherwise you will rob your magic of its power to succeed. When you are sated with this effort, raise your hand and pour out the accumulated light into the talisman. See it hover and play about it. Let the talisman absorb the light and look into the depths of the talisman and there see your will being accomplished. Know that it is true for there can be no other way. Pick up the talismanic figure and approach the east and say:

> 'Hear Me O Mizrach!
> Hear Me!
> For this talisman is duly consecrated to achieve (state your intent)
> For as I do will
> So Mote It BE!'

Repeat this at the south changing the name Mizrach to Darom, the west to Mearab, and the north to Tzaphon. These are the old names from medieval ritual for the elemental quarters. Face the element that you have been working with and give thanks such as:

> 'I do give thanks to the Holy Element ... (state which one) and to the mighty names (God Name)
> and to the Holy Archangel... (state name)
> and to the Angel of ... (state element and then Angel Name) and to the Holy King... (name)
> for assisting me with this, my act of magic.
> Let there be peace, grace and harmony between us now and for evermore
> for I too am a servant of the God Most High!'

Place the talisman on the altar and cover with a cloth, preferably one of silk. At this stage with the closing rite you do not want to banish the energies aroused which will make your working pointless if this happens. Gazing at the talisman bring your hand down sharply as if to cut an imaginary link to the talismanic figure. The talisman is now an independent being, a creature in its own right. Facing east declare the following:

> 'Non Nobis Domini, Non Nobis, Sed nomini tuo da honorum, Propter begnignitatem tuam, Propter fide tuam.'
> (Not unto us O Lord, Not unto us, but unto thy name be the glory for your mercy and faith.)

Close now with the LBRP and declare:

> 'Domini Unam Est!'
> (The Lord is One)

The talisman must be kept safe and out of sight, it could be hidden in a small envelope and housed within your wallet if it is for yourself; or placed in the vicinity of somebody if it is to influence them. However the talisman may need to be retrieved or destroyed, and to do that, to de-activate it, visualise the energies are leaving it as you return it to its element and declare that this is so and give thanks for its help.

Another means of working with the sigils would be to inscribe them on a candle that is coloured suitably for the work, consecrate it according to our arte and let it burn out with the intent that as it does so one's will is released. This could be used in a complex rite or something that is simple or adapted from the rites of modern witchcraft as with the use of the mirror which has been previously mentioned.

Of the Use of the Sigils as given:

Traditionally the sigils that can be created from the geomantic symbols have had the following meanings attributed to them which gives a guide to the traditional usage.

Good for voyages and quick results	Acquisitio, Caput Draconis, Fortuna Major/Minor and Laetitia.
Good by land	Populus, Laetitia, Albus, Conjunctio and Via
Good by water	Populus, Laetitia, Puella, Albus and Acquisitio
Slow for voyages but profitable	Carcer and Puella
Evil for travel	Rubeus, Conjunctio, Populus and Tristitia
Robbing by the way	Cauda Draconis and Rubeus
Evil and good to cause fear	Cauda Draconis and Rubeus
Good for honours and integrity	Acquisitio, Fortuna Major/Minor, Laetitia, Albus, Caput Draconis and Conjunctio
Good to have liberty and to come out of prison	Fortuna Minor and Via

Mean to come out of prison	Carcer, Rubeus, Puella and Albus
Good for body	Populus, Conjunctio, and Fortuna Minor
Mean for body	Albus, Puella and Puer
Evil for body	Carcer, Rubeus and Amissio
Good for women (pregnant)	Amissio, Fortuna Minor, Via and Laetitia
Child will die	Tristitia
Mean for child birth	Amissio, Cauda Draconis and Populus
Better than before	Via, Caput Draconis, Laetitia, Tristitia
Marriage Good	Fortuna Major, Laetitia, Caput Draconis
Marriage for evil	Amissio, Via and Rubeus
Good for dread and fear	Amissio, Via, Cauda Draconis and Puer
Good for women's love	Laetitia, Caput Draconis, Puer, Fortuna Major
Evil for women's love	Amissio, Via, Rubeus, Cauda Draconis and Carcer
Good to recover things	Acquisito, Caput Draconis, Conjunctio
Good to recover things stolen	Acquisitio, Caput Draconis, Conjunctio, Puella Medium

Evil for things stolen	Fortuna Minor, Laetitia, Cauda Draconis, Populus and Via
Good for shipping	Acquisitio, Laetitia, Fortuna Major/Minor, Via
Medium	Cauda Draconis
Evil for shipping	Ammisio, Carcer and Tristitia
Good to remove	Cauda Draconis, Rubeus, Puer and Carcer
Evil figures signifying evil	Via, Carcer, Puer, Amissio, Tristitia, Cauda Draconis and Rubeus
Figures of chastity and virginity	Albus, Fortune Major, Laetitia, Carcer, Tristia, Puella and Caput Draconis
Figure of incontinence and lechery	Puer, Cauda Draconis, Amissio, Rubeus, Conjunctio, Acquisitio and Fortuna Major
Figures signifying peace	Fortuna Major, Acquisitio, Caput Draconis, Laetitia, Albus, and Puella
Figures of loss	Carcer, Albus, Laetitia, Populus, Via, Amissio, Puer, Rubeus, Fortuna Minor, and Cauda Draconis
Figures of gain	Acquisito, Fortuna Major, Tristitia, Puella and Caput Draconis
Figures of nobility	Acquisitio, Laetitia, Puella, Fortuna Major/Minor
Figures of ignobility	Tristitia, Carcer, Via, Cauda Draconis, and Conjunctio
Figures of life	Albus, Fortuna Major, Laetitia, Puella, Acquisitio, Populus, Caput Draconis and Via
Figures of death	Tristitia, Cauda Draconis, Carcer, Rubeus, Puer, Conjunctio, Acquisitio and Amissio

Figures of avarice and covetousness	Tristitia, Carcer, Conjunctio, Fortuna Major
Figure of justice	Puer
Figure of prudence	Acquisitio
Figure of fortitude	Amissio
Good to buy cattle	Puella, Populus and Caput Draconis
Loss to buy cattle	Tristitia and Carcer
Figure of temperance	Conjunctio

Of the elemental workings:

Mizrach (air):

'Such a fire existeth, extending through the rushing of air, or even a fire formless whence cometh the image of a voice, or even a flashing light, abounding, revolving, whirling forth, crying aloud!'

Talismanic Figure of Air:

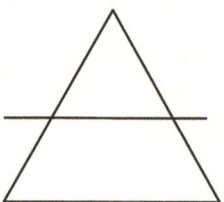

God Name:	SHADDAI EL CHAI
	(sha-die el kye)
Archangel:	Raphael
Angel:	Chasan
King:	Paralda
Spiritual creatures:	Sylphs

'O thou holy ones of the eastern quarter Mizrach Hear Me!
For I do invoke thee this day By thy holy and mighty name SHADDAI EL CHAI!
Almighty Living God!
And in the name of thy potent archangel Raphael!
Let the energies of Air assist me with this my holy act of magic!'

AIR TALISMAN

Sigils from Albus and Fortuna Minor

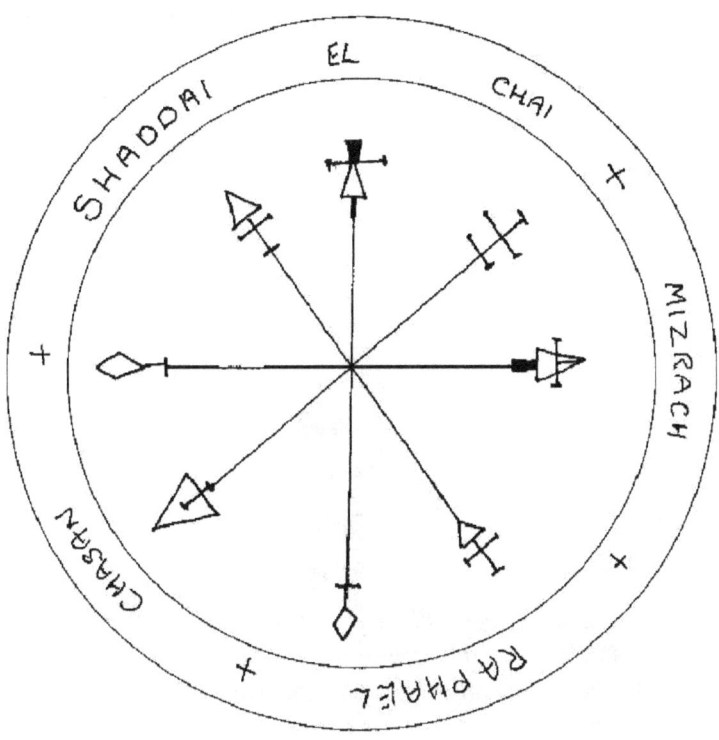

Darom (fire):

'And when after all the phantoms have vanished thou shalt see the holy and formless fire, the fire that flashes through the hidden depths of the universe, hear thou the voice of fire!'

Talismanic Figure of Fire:

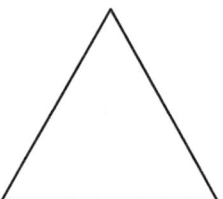

God Name:	YHVH TZABAOTH
	(yah-veh tza-vay-ot)
Archangel:	Mikael
Angel:	Aral
King:	Djinn
Spiritual Creatures:	Salamanders

'O thou holy powers of the south Darom!
For thee I invoke this day
By the mighty and holy name unto which thou art subject YHVH TZABAOTH!
Lord of Armies!
And in the power of thine Archangel Mikael!
Aid me this day O holy element fire With this mine act of magic!'

FIRE TALISMAN

Sigils from Fortuna Major and Acquisitio

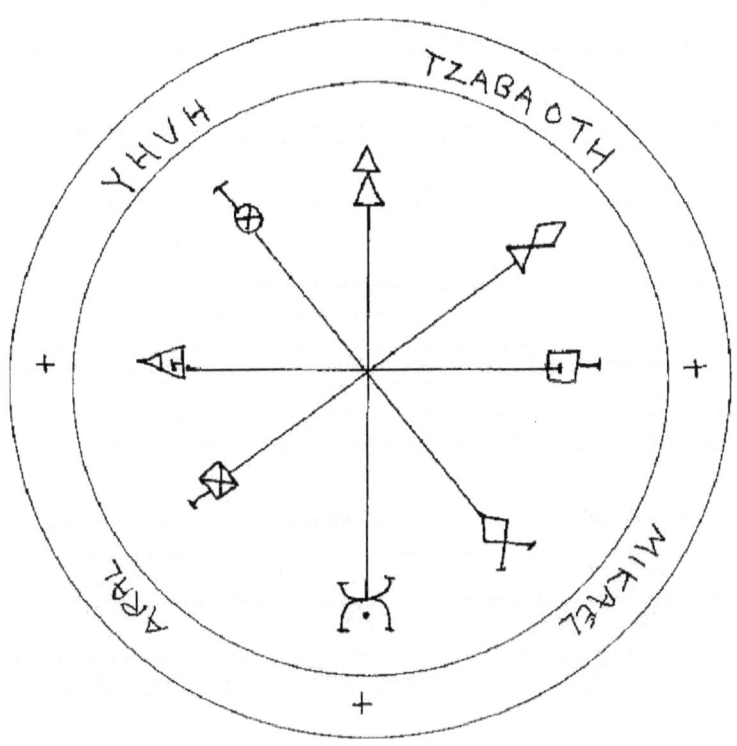

Mearab (water):

'And Elohim said: Let us make Adam in our image, after our likeness, and let him have dominion over the fish of the sea!'

Talismanic figure of water:

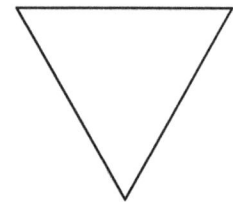

God Name:	ELOHIM TZABAOTH
	(el-o-heem tza-vay-ot)
Archangel:	Gabriel
Angel:	Taliahad
King:	Niksa
Spiritual creatures:	Undines

'Hear Me Mearab!
Thy holy powers of ebb and flow For I do invoke thee
By thine holy and potent names ELOHIM TZABAOTH!
Elohim of Hosts!
And by the might of the Holy Archangel Gabriel!
Let the powers of thy kingdom be obedient unto the mighty names and assist me with this mine holy act of magic!'

WATER TALISMAN

Sigils of Populus

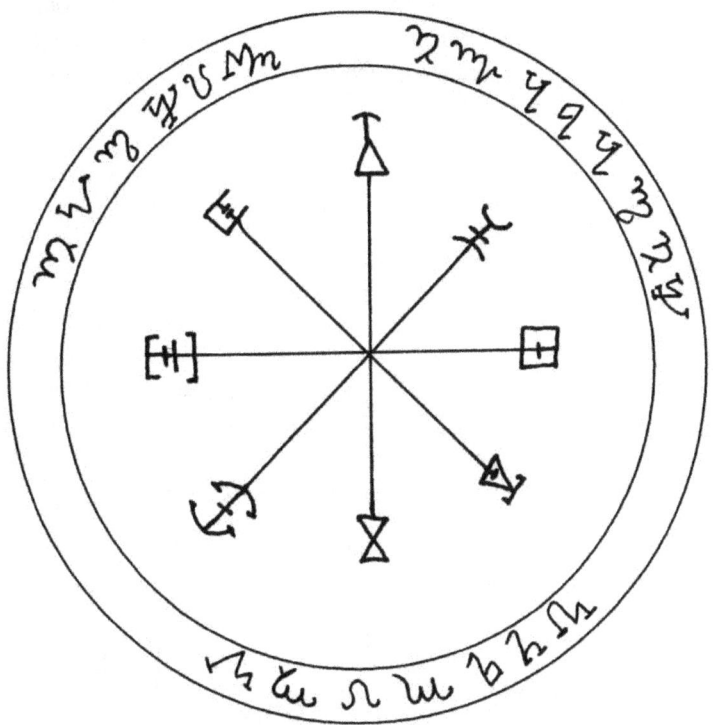

Tzaphon (earth):

'Stoop not down into that darkly splendid world wherein continually lieth a faithless depth and Hades wrapped in gloom, delighting in unintelligible images, precipitous, winding, a black ever rolling abyss, ever espousing a body unluminous, formless and void!'

Talismanic figure of earth:

▽

God Name:	ADONAI HA-ARETZ
	(ah-do-nye ha-a-retz)
Archangel:	Uriel
Angel:	Phorlak
Spiritual creature:	Gnomes

'Mighty Tzaphon, the giver of plenty Hear Me!
For in and by thy holy names ADONAI HA-ARETZ!
Lord of the Earth I invoke thee!
And by the might of thy holy archangel Auriel!
I do invoke, summon and stir thee up O element earth!
Assist me with this my holy act of magic!'

EARTH TALISMAN

Sigils of Caput Draconis and Conjunctio

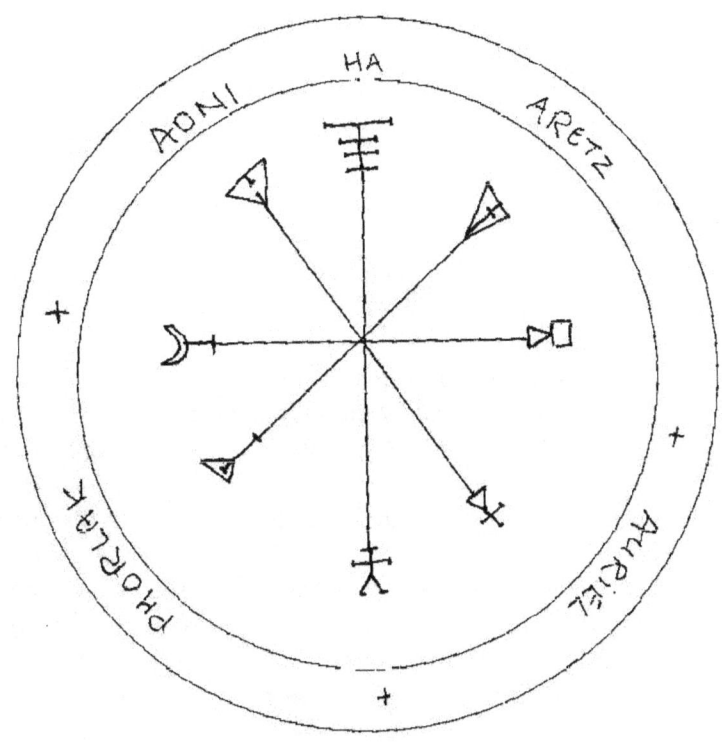

CHAPTER SEVEN

'Doors of Perception'

The geomantic symbols have a little known but powerful use that they can be put to: the exploration of the subtle levels of being. In modern times the practice of using symbols to explore levels of consciousness has been well covered by several practitioners. This practice has been used by the psychologist Jung to good effect, who discovered it by accident. One day he was travelling up an escalator and a poster on the wall had an alpine scene displayed. Looking at it he wondered what was on the other side of the hill. Then he suddenly realised he had projected his consciousness into the picture and was walking through the valley that it showed to see what was on the other side. Snapping out of the daydream he realised the importance that this could have for exploring symbols and the like. What he had done was not new; this technique had been used by Jesuit priests to explore biblical scenes. It was used to build up regular scenes from the life of Jesus and then imagine that they were in the picture and interrelating with the figure therein.

This method of consciousness projection was also used by the Golden Dawn, a late 19th-20th century magical order who have influenced Western Occultism ever since. Their method was to use symbols relating to the Holy Kabbalah, the elements, or tarot cards and was one completely different to the modern New Age approach, which has been adopted by the neo-pagan movement. The common practice of having someone reading a descriptive passage with everyone following it in their imaginations (*'As we walk along the beach, the friendly dolphins wave back...'*) is a pointless exercise as it produces nothing, no understanding or perceptions of any worth. This is a technique that I find meaningless and is a watered-down version of traditional practice.

Within the Western Magical Traditions the practice of working with symbols by the use of ritual techniques and the building up of them in the imagination, walking into them and experiencing the events that unfold, has been part of training systems for a long time, and it is one that can be extremely potent, particularly when repeated over time.

The use of geomantic symbols for this type of magical work is simple but effective. Firstly I would suggest that you wash and change into something suitable as this helps to create the right frame of mind. After all you are doing something different from the everyday. Having chosen which symbols that you are going to explore, you could cast your rune staves to divine which door to work with for this. Use a suitable incense and candle light which will greatly enhance the atmosphere and help create the right moods as you endeavour to 'connect' with the energies involved.

Settle the atmosphere by using the Lesser Banishing Ritual of the Pentagram, with this working the use of fire and water for consecrating the working space will not be needed. Use words of your own and state clearly what the working is about. Sitting comfortably build up the symbol in your imagination as a door before you. Let the scene be clear and strong. The skills of visualisation will take time to build up therefore regular practice will help. Imagine that an invoking pentagram forms over the door to open it, and declare silently to yourself that the door is opening, thus allowing you entry. Now imagine that you are walking into the scene that unfolds before you. Do not speak to anyone until you are spoken to first. Observe the scenes and events that arise before you. Sometimes you can be shown events or answers to problems, or even be given information about all manner of things that are relevant in some way to you or to your understanding of the magical artes. Other times things can seem to be quite trivial. Some doorways will be more relevant to you, and some more potent than others - you will have to accept them on their terms and not yours. With regular use an empathy will develop with the energies they contain which will aid you with working with them either as a divination system or through the spellcraft that I have outlined. If nothing else they will improve your self-discipline, concentration and visualisation skills.

When you come back on the path, making sure it is the one that you entered by, close the door behind you, and see a banishing pentagram forming over the door to close it. Stand up and stamp your foot to indicate that you are back in the everyday world. Give thanks for the experience and to those energies that have assisted you and close with the Lesser Banishing Ritual of the Pentagram . This work can be performed over several weeks, by performing one working a week, or even two, if they are not affecting you too much, and if time and commitment allow. They can prove very profound and produce many relevant insights.

In themselves they can become an initiation into geomantic magic in their own right and are well worth performing. Whilst sometimes they may not seem to be having any effect on the mundane levels or to be producing results in the short term, do not doubt them, for on the subtle levels you may be sure that the call of your working has gone out and that the magic will surely answer. These workings will need to be done many times and with persistence they will release their secrets if you can understand them. In my own experience of such workings I have found that whilst in the scene and whilst things are being explained to you, everything can seem crystal clear, but when you are back in the everyday world then you can have difficulty trying to put into words that which you have experienced. I have found through my own experiences that you are more likely to grasp intuitively the meanings of the visions shown rather than someone spelling things out clearly for you in simple terms. This type of magic will, if practiced regularly, greatly improve your magical skills as it uses and develops many of the abilities that are needed for the successful practice of our arte.

FINIS

Index

A

acacia 36
Acquisitio..20, 29, 48, 49, 50, 51, 55
Agrippa, Cornelius 12
air 17, 19, 21, 34, 35, 39, 43, 44, 52
Albus 17, 48, 49, 50, 53
Amissio 17, 49, 50, 51
angelica 36
aqua aurum.. 34, *See* gold water
Aquarius 15, 21, 34, 35
Aral 54
Aries 16, 34
Auriel 43, 58

B

Bartzabel 16, 20
brandy 34, 35, 36

C

camphor 24
Cancer 18, 24, 35
Capricorn 21, 35, 42
Caput Draconis 23, 48, 49, 50, 51, 59
caraway 35
Carcer 21, 30, 48, 49, 50, 51
carnation 35
Cauda Draconis..... 22, 48, 49, 50
cedar 20, 22, 23
chamomile 36
Chasan 52

Chasmondai 18, 24
cinnamon 36
civet 21
condensers 33, 34, 37
Conjunctio.19, 48, 49, 50, 51, 59
coriander 35
cucumber 36
Culpeper, Nicholas 12

D

Darom 47, 54
Daughters 26, 30
Djinn 54
dragon's blood 16, 20, 22, 34, 36

E

earth 17, 21, 23, 33, 36, 39, 42, 43, 44, 58

F

fire . 16, 18, 20, 22, 34, 35, 37, 38, 44, 45, 52, 54, 61
Fludd, Robert 12
Fortuna Major.18, 23, 48, 49, 50, 51, 55
Fortuna Minor 48, 49, 50, 53
Fortune, Dion 41
frankincense ...15, 18, 23, 34, 35, 36

G

Gabriel 43, 56
garlic 34

Gemini 15, 17, 34, 35
gnomes.. 58
gold water 34, 35, 36
Golden Dawn............................... 60
Granddaughters 26

H

hazel 14, 35
Heydon, John 12
Hismael.................................. 20, 22
house... 16, 17, 18, 20, 23, 29, 30, 31, 32, 35, 42, 44

J

Judge... 29
juniper.. 35
Jupiter 20, 22

K

Kabbalah 41, 60
karaya.. 35
Kedemel 17, 19

L

Laetitia 22, 28, 48, 49, 50
lavender 17, 36
LBRP........... 42, 44, 47, 61, 62, *See* Lesser Banishing Ritual of the Pentagram
lemon balm................................ 35
Leo 18, 23, 34
Lesser Banishing Ritual of the Pentagram............................ 42
Libra....................... 15, 19, 34, 35
lily 36
lime 36
lotus.. 35

M

Mars 16, 20
Mearab................................. 47, 56
Mercury 17, 19

Mikael................................... 43, 54
Mizrach 47, 52
Moon ... 14, 15, 18, 22, 23, 24, 34, 35, 36, 37, 42, 44
Mothers 25, 26, 27, 28, 30, 31
musk... 19
mustard 34
myrrh..................................... 21, 22

N

nettles 36
Nieces................... 26, 28, 30, *See* Granddaughters
Niksa 56

O

onion 34
opopanax.................................... 20
opposite 32

P

Paralda 52
parsley 35
patchouli.................................... 36
peppercorn 34
peppermint............................... 36
Philtron Animato...................... 33
Phorlak.. 58
Pisces..................................... 22, 35
plantain 35
poplar.. 36
Populus....... 18, 48, 49, 50, 51, 57
Puella................ 19, 48, 49, 50, 51
Puer................... 16, 49, 50, 51

R

Raphael................................ 43, 52
rose 17, 23, 35
Rubeus..................20, 48, 49, 50

S

sage 36

Sagittarius............................ 20, 34
salamanders................................ 54
Saturn.................................. 21, 30
Scorpio................................ 20, 35
sextile.. 32
Sorath.................................. 18, 23
square.. 32
storax... 36
Sun....................................... 18, 23
sylphs... 52

T

Taliahad...................................... 56
talisman.................. 41, 44, 46, 47
Taphthartharath................. 17, 19
Taurus............................ 17, 35, 42
Theomagia................................... 13
trine.. 32
Tristitia........21, 30, 48, 49, 50, 51
Tzaphon................................ 47, 58

U

undines....................................... 56

Universal Condenser............... 34
Uriel.. 58

V

Venus................................... 17, 19
Via..............................24, 48, 49, 50
violet... 36
Virgo............................... 19, 35, 42

W

water ... 15, 18, 20, 22, 24, 34, 35, 36, 37, 38, 39, 40, 43, 44, 45, 46, 48, 56, 61
white sandalwood.................... 24
willow.................................... 35, 36
Witness...................................... 29
wort cauldron...................... 34, 36

Y

Yesod... 41

Z

Zazel... 21

FOUNDATIONS OF PRACTICAL SORCERY

A seven-volume set of magical treatises, unabridged, comprising:

Vol. I - Liber Noctis

A Handbook of the Sorcerous Arte

Liber Noctis explores the attitudes, training and preparation required for success in ritual, and, as the title suggests, does not shy away from the 'darker' aspects of magic. Practical, experiential, lucid and non-judgmental, this book lays the groundwork for the successful study and practice of sorcery in the modern world.

Vol. II - Ars Salomonis

Being of that Hidden Arte of Solomon the King

Ars Salomonis is a practical manual for working with the talismanic figures found in the Key of Solomon, the most significant of all grimoires. Including two methods for empowering and activating the planetary pentacles, the author makes this vital work safely accessible to beginners. It is an ideal entranceway into the grimoire tradition.

Vol. III - Ars Geomantica

Being an account and rendition of the Arte of Geomantic Divination and Magic

Ars Geomantica explores the medieval system of Geomancy, one of the simplest and most practical of the divinatory arts. The inclusion of detailed instructions on the creation of geomantic staves, elemental fluid condensers, and talismanic construction and consecration make this work a superb introduction to an extensive assortment of magical and divinatory principles.

Vol. IV - Ars Theurgia Goetia

Being an account and rendition of the Arte and Praxis of the Conjuration of some of the Spirits of Solomon

Ars Theurgia Goetia presents a precise and practical guide to working with the spirits of this neglected text from the Solomonic grimoire cycle, the Theurgia-Goetia, giving the full seals of the spirits for the first time. The complete ritual sequence of preparation, conjuration, and license to depart is lucidly demonstrated, making this work suitable for both the beginner and the experienced practitioner.

Vol. V - Otz Chim

The Tree of Life

Otz Chim is a practical exploration of the magic of the Kabbalistic Tree of Life, the glyph that concentrates the essence of magic and mysticism within the Western Mystery Tradition. This book focuses on lesser-known aspects such as the angels associated with the paths, their seals, and invocations and includes the previously unavailable Massa Aborum Vitae.

Vol. VI - Ars Speculum

Being an Instruction on the Arte of using Mirrors and Shewstones in Magic

Ars Speculum is a concise and practical work on the use of mirrors and shewstones in magic. In it the author explores skrying and working with the four elements of air, fire, water and earth - both with elemental condensers and different elemental creatures. Other techniques include contacting other levels of being, the conjuration of spirits, binding and ligature, and healing and protection.

Vol. VII - Liber Terriblis

Being an Instruction on the seventy-two Spirits of the Goetia

Liber Terribilis is a practical study of how to work with the seventy-two spirits of the infamous seventeenth-century Grimoire, the Goetia. It also explores the vital and often neglected use of the seventy-two binding angels of the Great Name of God, the Schemhamphorasch. This volume will be of value to all levels of students and practitioners of the grimoire traditions, being based upon the work of a small group of occultists who have explored it in practice.

More information available on the Avalonia website-
www.avaloniabooks.co.uk

Or write to:
BM Avalonia
London
WC1N 3XX
England, United Kingdom

Expanding the Esoteric Horizons ...

Avalonia *is an independent publisher producing outstanding and innovative books which push the boundaries of their subjects and illuminate the spirit of the sacred in its many manifestations.*

Explore some of the other works on the occult, mythology and magic published by Avalonia at:

www.avaloniabooks.co.uk

Readers who found Foundations of Practical Sorcery of interest, is likely to enjoy:

A Collection of Magical Secrets & a Treatise of mixed Cabalah by Stephen Skinner and David Rankine

Climbing the Tree of Life by David Rankine

Living Theurgy by Jeffrey S. Kupperman

Practical Elemental Magick by Sorita d'Este and David Rankine

The Book of Gold by David Rankine & Paul Harry Barron (trans.)

The Book of Treasure Spirits, edited by David Rankine

The Complete Grimoire of Pope Honorius by David Rankine & Paul Harry Barron (trans.)

The Cunning Man's Handbook by Jim Baker

The Grimoire of Arthur Gauntlet by David Rankine

Thoth by Lesley Jackson

Thracian Magic by Georgi Mishev

Wicca Magickal Beginnings by Sorita d'Este and David Rankine

www.ingramcontent.com/pod-product-compliance
Lightning Source LLC
LaVergne TN
LVHW091552070426
835507LV00010B/808